IT'S FUN TO LEARN ABOUT
SCIENCE

Arianne Holden
Consultant: Sharon Whittingham

ARMADILLO

NOTES

This book introduces children to essential first science concepts in a lively and stimulating way that is guaranteed to capture their imagination.

Learning the basics
This book shows children that science is part of their everyday lives, as they throw a ball, push a truck or whizz down a slide. There are plenty of simple experiments and investigations that will strengthen children's understanding, encouraging them to find out more.

Reading together
Most children benefit from adult help when reading a book. Do not expect a child to grasp all the information at once! It is better to look at one concept at a time, and allow a few days for the information to be absorbed.

Talking it through
Talk about the things you have found out together. Make everyday activities into a science adventure – bathtime is perfect for talking about floating and sinking, or hot and cold, and cooking lunch is a chance to think about melting, heating and how cooking something can change it.

Answering questions
Ask your child questions and encourage him or her to answer. Do not worry if the answers are wrong – making mistakes is part of the learning process. The most important thing is that your child feels confident and willing to try.

Checking your child's understanding
You can check your child's understanding of simple science by asking questions like – It is cold today? Which clothes should you put on? What will happen when I throw this ball? Praise your child when he or she answers questions correctly.

CONTENTS

Things that move

Things can move quickly or slowly, forwards or backwards, or even round and round!

Beep! Beep! Beep!

Ben and Sam move fast, but Jane is too slow!

I can move forwards ...

... and backwards.

You can move in lots of different ways. Can you make ...

... tiny steps?

... giant steps?

up and down

How do these things move?

around and around

Did you know?

The sleek cheetah is the fastest animal on Earth.

4

Wheels are round.

Wheels help things move smoothly and easily.

This wheelbarrow is easy to move but ...

... this one isn't. Can you see what's missing?

All these things have wheels.

bicycle

toy tractor

skateboard

The fire engine will move quickly down this slope ...

... but faster down this slope. Do you know why?

Try this!

Make a pull-along cart

1. Trace around a cup to make four wheels. Cut them out.

2. Push two pencils through two wheels. Fix them with modelling clay.

3. Make four holes in a small box. Push pencils into the holes.

4. Fix wheels to the other end of the pencils with modelling clay. Tie string to one end.

Push and pull

When you push or pull, you can make something move.

pushing a go-cart

Pull, Emma ...

Pull hard, Emma and Sam ...

Pull harder, Emma, Sam and Anna ...

How do you make ...

... a toy dog move?

... a scooter move?

Hooray! They've done it.

6

Try this!

Magic bucket

Pour a little water into a bucket. Swing it round and round, with a straight arm.

The water will be pushed into the bucket, and it won't fall out!

Ted has to push and pull to make the swing move.

Wheee! This is fun!

Push and pull some clay to make a fierce dragon!

When you get dressed, you ...

... pull up your socks

... push your feet into your shoes

... push your hands into your gloves

... pull on a t-shirt

... pull down your hat

Pull your lips and push out your tongue. What a funny face!

7

Floating and sinking

Some things, like boats and ducks, float on water. Other things sink.

Diving Bear will find out which things sink.

Try this!

Make a sailing boat

1. Cut a triangular sail from card. Glue on a straw.

2. Fold the card over the straw. Fix with adhesive tape.

3. Press modelling clay into the base of a tub.

4. Push the straw into the modelling clay.

A sailing boat floats.

Ducks float on water ...

... and so does Ted's rubber inner tube

Diving Bear finds things that sink ...

... sinking gold coins

... an anchor

... a pirate's sunken treasure chest

... sand, pebbles and shells

Drop lots of different things into some water. Which ones float? Which ones sink? This is called an investigation.

pencils

socks

wooden blocks

Draw what happens on a sheet of paper.

sink float

plastic toy

pebbles

ball

clay

balloon

apple

banana

leaves

flower

feather

Balloons like to float. Push a small balloon ...

... and a big balloon under water.

Which one is easier to push?

9

Air and wind

You can't see air, but it's all around you.
There is even air inside your body!

Have you ever ...

... blown bubbles full of air?

... seen bubbles of air in a drink?

... pumped air into a balloon?

The air in this bag came from John's lungs.

... blown out birthday candles?

When air moves, it can make other things move. Wind is moving air.

On a windy day ...

... leaves flutter

... hair gets blown about

... a windsock fills with air

... a kite flies

10

Try this!

Make a whizzing balloon

1. Thread a straw on to a long piece of string.

2. Inflate a long balloon. Stop the air escaping with a clamp.

3. Tape the straw to the balloon.

4. Ask friends to hold the ends of the string. Release the clamp. The balloon will whizz away!

These things have air inside them –

arm floats

soccer ball

balloons

bouncing ball

Pretend to be the wind. Blow on to the sails to make the boats move.

An umbrella can be turned inside out by the wind.

Gravity

Things fall to the ground because of an invisible force called gravity.

Going up is hard work ...

... but sliding down is easy!

Wheee!

What goes up ... must come down!

When you jump into the air ...

... gravity pulls you down.

A slinky spring slinks down.

These toys work because of gravity.

The marble rolls down the marble run.

Gravity pulls the woodpecker down the stick.

*tap
tap*

12

Did you know?

There is no gravity in Space. If you threw a ball, it would float away from you.

What happens if Peter stops juggling?

Orange juice!

Which of these things falls the fastest and reaches the ground first?

A piece of paper or ...

... a ball of paper?

Two identical balls?

A feather or ...

... a plastic toy?

Will the ball roll up or down the slope?

Try this!

Make a gravity painting

1. Mix up runny paints and pour spoonfuls on to card.

2. Tip the card side to side, and backwards and forwards. The paint will run and make patterns.

Balance

If something is balanced,
it will not topple over.

Roll up and watch Freddy Frog
and his friends balance ...

One of these towers
will fall over because
it is not balanced.

Do you know
which one?

... a spinning
plate

... two cherry cakes

... on one
leg with
eyes shut

... on a drum

... on stepping stones

... on a tightrope

Try this!

Make a stand-up person

1. Fold a large rectangular piece of card in half.

2. Draw a person on it. The head is near the fold.

3. Cut it out, but do not cut along the fold.

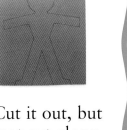

4. Draw a face. Open the card to make your stand-up person balance.

Which of these is balanced?

The ice cream or ...

... the wizard's hat?

This chair ...

... or this wobbly one?

This tower ...

... or this one?

Spin around in a large, open space to make yourself dizzy.

When you stop, is it hard to keep your balance?

This seesaw ...

... or this seesaw?

15

Hot and cold

Hot and cold things feel different to touch. Some things change when they are heated up or cooled down.

To make yourself warm ...

phew!

You sweat when you're hot.

brrr!

You shiver when you're cold.

... rub your hands together

... use a hot water bottle

... wrap up well

Stay cool with a breeze from a fan.

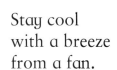

Some food has to be kept cold in a refrigerator.

Yuck, warm sour milk!

Try this!

Crunchy chocolate cakes

1. Wash your hands. Break 125g/4¼oz of chocolate into pieces. Ask a grown-up to help you melt it.

2. Mix the melted chocolate with 2 cups of crunchy cereal.

3. Spoon it into paper cases. Place them in the refrigerator to go hard.

Here are some things that change when heated or cooled. Take care! Hot things can burn you.

Cheese melts ...

... when it is cooked.

Chocolate melts in your warm fingers.

Chocolate cake batter becomes ... cooked cake.

Frozen water is solid.

Melted ice is liquid.

Butter ... melts on hot toast.

Yummy ice cream ...

Cook a raw egg to make ... a scrambled egg ... or a fried egg.

... melts when it gets warm.

Your body

Your body has lots of different parts.
You can see some parts, but others
are hidden under the skin.

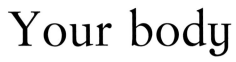

head

Hard nails protect
your fingers.

fingers

arm

hair

hand

elbow

chest

Can you
feel your
hard skull ...

waist

hip

bottom

... and the
bones in
your knees?

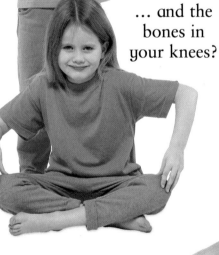

leg

knee

ankle

foot

toes

There are lots of bones in your feet.

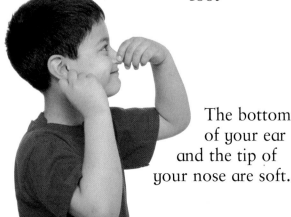

The bottom
of your ear
and the tip of
your nose are soft.

18

Under your skin are muscles and bones. They help you to ...

... climb

... eat

... paint

... run

What else can you do with your body?

Your skin can make a ...

... funny face.

Your heart pumps blood around your body.

thump thump

Have you ever listened to your heart?

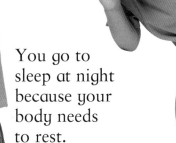

You go to sleep at night because your body needs to rest.

Did you know?

Your brain tells your body what to do. It is inside your head. Your brain weighs about the same as 12 apples.

19

Growing

All living things grow and get bigger. To grow, they need food, water and sunlight.

big girl

little girl

Look at how much Fred has grown!

baby girl

Fluffy chicks grow up to be chickens.

Puppies grow up to be dogs.

A hairy caterpillar goes to sleep in a cocoon and changes into a butterfly.

When some animals grow, they change completely!

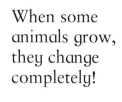
20

Try this!

Growing a bean seed

1. Get some bean seeds.

2. Push the seeds into some soil.

3. Put in a sunny spot and water each day.

4. Watch your bean seeds grow.

You wouldn't eat soil for dinner, but growing plants get their food from soil.

Look at how a hyacinth plant grows. Where are its roots?

It starts as a bulb.

It then grows a leafy stem.

Leaves and a flower bud grow.

Leaves grow taller and the flower opens.

Frogs lay eggs called spawn. Tadpoles hatch from eggs and grow into frogs. Croak!

21

Touching and feeling

You feel with your skin. You can learn about things by the way they feel.

strawberry

orange

banana

What do these fruits feel like?

pineapple

mango

grapes

Ouch!

A prickly holly bush.

Your sense of touch warns you of danger.

We like to wear things that feel nice. Which of these things would you wear?

A soft **sweater** or ...

... a scratchy one?

Try this!

A feely picture

1. Glue felt, foil and abrasive paper on to card.

2. Use cotton wool, sponge, card and shells to make a seaside scene.

Fluffy grey slippers or ...

... scrubbing brush slippers?

22

... under your arms?

Are you
ticklish ...

... under
your chin?

... on your feet?

When your hands are cold it is hard to pick things up.

Which is more
ticklish ...

... the back
of your hand ...

... or the palm
of your hand?

Ask a grown-up to
help you do this.

Put one
foot in
cold water.

Put the
other foot
in warm
water.

Wait for a little
while before standing
in lukewarm water.

How does each foot feel?

23

Sound and hearing

Our ears help us to hear sounds.
Sounds are made by moving air.

I can
hear you.

I can hear
you too.

What a lot of noise!

brrr
brrr

What sounds
do these noisy
things make?

jingle
jingle

honk!
honk!
honk!

bang!
crash!

toot
toot

Did you know?

Elephants a have excellent hearing.
They can hear one another from
at least 4km (2½ miles) away.

Try this!

Sshh! A whispering game

1. Sit your friends in a circle. Make up a silly rhyme.

2. Whisper it to the friend sitting next to you.

3. Keep going until the whisper gets back to you. Is your silly rhyme still the same?

Record yourself talking and singing, then play it back.

Does it sound like you?

Your voice will travel through this tube.

Sounds can change. Try shouting into a bucket.

Your tongue helps you make sounds.

Sing with your tongue like this ... and then like this.

Does your voice sound different?

Making music

When air is squashed or moved it makes a noise. Different things are used to squash and move air to make music.

tap, **tap**, **tap** with my shoes

clap, clap, clap with my hands

on my guitar

twang

twang

maracas

thump

thump

thump

on the floor

xylophone

ting

ting

ting

on my triangle

castanets

recorder

drum

la

la

la

with my voice

You can make music using things in your home. You can make ...

... a loud sound

... low sounds

...or high sounds

... a quiet sound

... windy sounds

... lots of different tinkling sounds

... soft rustling noises

... very loud noises.

Try this!

Make a shaker

1. Get some dried lentils or beans.

2. Put them in a plastic cup.

3. Place a cup on top. Join them with tape.

4. Shake it up and down and side to side to make sounds.

Colour

Different colours are all around us. Some are light, and some are dark.

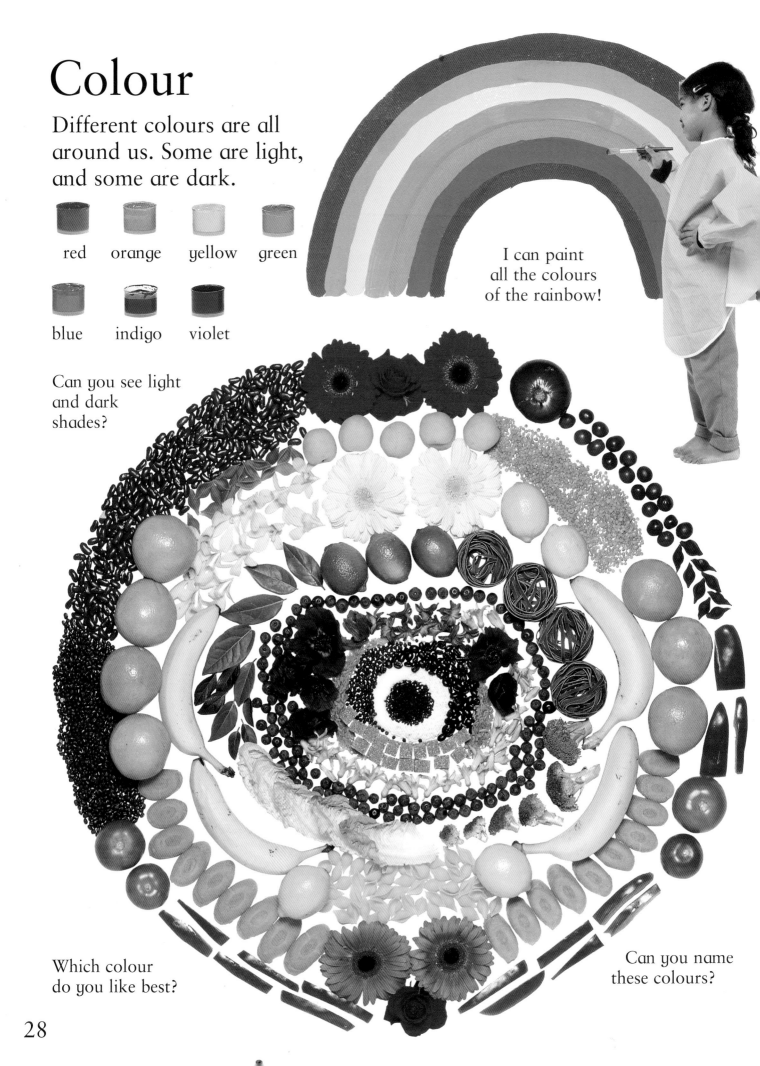

red   orange   yellow   green

blue   indigo   violet

I can paint all the colours of the rainbow!

Can you see light and dark shades?

Which colour do you like best?

Can you name these colours?

Use cellophane to make crazy glasses. What happens to the colours around you?

You can make lots of different shades by mixing red, yellow and blue.

Red and yellow make orange.

Red and blue make purple.

Blue and yellow make green.

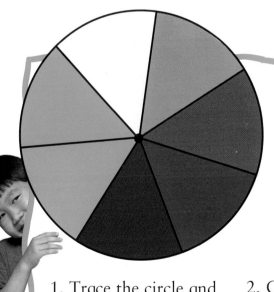

Try this!

Make a magic wheel

3. Spin the wheel. What colour is it?

1. Trace the circle and lines on to tracing paper. Transfer the tracing to a piece of white card.

2. Cut out the circle. Colour it in exactly as shown. Push a pencil through the middle.

Question and answer game

Answer the questions and then make your way through the wiggly maze to see if your answers are correct. Give yourself a point for every question you get right.

START

What happens if the popsicle gets warm?

John goes down the slide.

A dog.

It melts.

What does a puppy grow into?

What happens next?

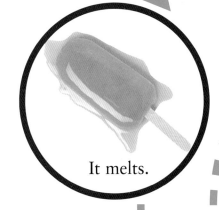

What happens when Sam blows on the candles?

The candles will go out.

What do red and yellow make?

Orange.

It falls down.

They make a loud noise.

What happens to the wobbly tower?

What happens to the apple?

What can a seed grow into?

What happens when Tom bangs the cymbals?

It falls down. Crash!

Hooray, you've made it! How many points did you get?

FINISH

A plant.

31

This edition is published by Armadillo,
an imprint of Anness Publishing Ltd,
108 Great Russell Street,
London WC1B 3NA;
info@anness.com

www.annesspublishing.com; twitter: @Anness_Books

Anness Publishing has a new picture agency outlet
for images for publishing, promotions or advertising.
Please visit our website www.practicalpictures.com
for more information.

© Anness Publishing Ltd 2015

Publisher: Joanna Lorenz
Senior Editor: Felicity Forster
Educational Consultant: Sharon Whittingham BEd
Photography: John Freeman
Head Stylist: Melanie Williams
Stylist: Ken Campbell
Designer: Louise Millar, Mike Leaman Design Partners
Production Controller: Ben Worley

PUBLISHER'S NOTE
Although the advice and information in this book are
believed to be accurate and true at the time of going to
press, neither the authors nor the publisher can accept any
legal responsibility or liability for any errors or omissions
that may have been made nor for any inaccuracies nor for
any loss, harm or injury that comes about from following
instructions or advice in this book.

Manufacturer: Anness Publishing Ltd,
108 Great Russell Street, London WC1B 3NA, England
For Product Tracking go to: www.annesspublishing.com/tracking
Batch: 7555-23901-1127

ACKNOWLEDGEMENTS
The publisher would like to thank the following children for
appearing in this book: Ambika, April, Archie-Leigh, Ashley, Billy,
Callum, Cleo, Daisy, Faye, Georgina, Harriet, Holly, Irene, Jack,
Jonathon, Kadeem, Kitty, Lucie, Luke, Maddison, Matthew, Miriam,
Olivia, Philip, Rebekah, Rosanna, Safari, Saffron, Sumaya, Tom,
Zaafir, Zamour.

PICTURE CREDITS
b=bottom, t=top, c=centre, l=left, r=right
Jane Burton: 20cl; 21bc. Stephen Dalton, NHPA: 21bl;
21br. Jane Ellis: 20cr; 20c. Clem Haagner: 4br.
Papilio: 20bl; 20c. Science Photo Library: 13tl.